MW00772194

Make Me Your Own

Poems to the Divine Beloved

Tosha Silver

Copyright ©2013 Tosha Silver
Library of Congress Control Number: 2013942723
ISBN: 978-0-9836817-1-7
1st Printing 2013
2nd Printing 2017

Printed and bound in the USA.

Front Cover Photo by Donna Insalaco
Cover Design by Carlo Armintia
Typesetting & Print Production by Michael Fantasia & Matthew Klein

Urban Kali Publishing
3001 Bridgeway, Suite 277
Sausalito ,CA 94965

Dedicated to the radiant Goddess and God inside us all

Preface

Around 2000, I realized I'd been composing love poems to the Divine in my heart since I was very young but not writing them down. So one day I began.

This book is the result and was originally published in 2013. For several years it's been out of print, though I've secretly longed to bring it back to life. People have never stopped asking for it. So big thanks to my manager and friend Matt Klein who masterminded this reincarnation, complete with a refreshed cover and even an extra bonus chapter of recent poems.

In a way, it continues the love letter to the Inner Lord that began with the first book, *Outrageous Openness: Letting the Divine Take the Lead.*

May it inspire, deepen or begin your own love affair with that playful, radiant, all-knowing and mysterious One within.

May it lead you to bow once and for all to your own exquisite and deserving Self,

the One within who has been waiting forever for You

perhaps until …Right Now.

Contents

Marry me.

Marry me, God.

Marry me god, to myself. Marry me god, to myself,

and give me back to the world.

McCarty Baker

1.

PIERCING THE SOUL

HOPELESSLY DEVOTED

what's funny is everyone
worships Something all day,

even the coldest fish

rabid devotion swims
in the blood
like corpuscles

of Light

people just make
small gods

of their partners
or kids

dreams or
desires

power
or money

being mad
or being liked

their worries, fears
or doubts,

regrets or pain

so why not
just make

an all-consuming,
shining

Deity of

Love?

FEROCIOUS HAND

Never doubt
what your own

wise heart

guides you to do

whether the action
be small or grand

and though some may
criticize or even mock

your way.

Fear not.

For when your heart speaks,
your own listening

is a supreme act
of devotion

And an invisible ferocious hand
will steady you

hold you up

make clear your route

until the time is right,

then fling open

with flagrant, festive
abandon

any door

that is

still

shut

PIERCING THE SOUL

This moon

a pearl-handled dagger of light

piercing the soul
wide
wide
open

it says

you've done enough
now just let go

receive

listen inside

to all You knew

you always knew

before others
trained you

to

forget

COCONUT

don't tell me

how well you conjure

dream

or list your wishes

for ghosts to grant
on Full Moons

or how you
manifested that mate

in a month

or that parking space

in a jam

or how you always get
whatever you want

whenever you want it

cuz honey
I still
don't care.

You can
spend
a whole life

chasing This
or That

when instead

You could be
a coconut

cracked by
God's own hand

and splashed
on this earth

like holy
milk

FOR THOSE WHO
SO ODDLY THOUGHT
THEY WEREN'T ENOUGH

Please change me

Divine Beloved

into One who can feel

wildly open to receiving

Let me know my own
value, beauty

and worthiness

without question

And let me allow others

the supreme pleasure

of giving to me.

O let me know how to receive

in every possible way!

Pelt me with miracles

like rain soaking a
cracked desert floor.

Caress my soul
with Your grace.

Steep me in Your Love
like peaches in wine.

Melt my heart
Melt my heart
Melt my heart

and

Change me into One

who can forgive

completely

so I may carry your Light

with abandon.

Let me accept
myself in every

possible way

for I am utterly

and
shamelessly

Your
Very

Own

II.

ROMANCING THE VOID

THE KISS

Since the Divine
will never
be closer

than She is
this moment

Her kiss
never waits 'til

you meet
your soulmate

have a baby

or adopt that stray dog

No need to nab
the perfect handstand

or hope that Venus
might finally submit

one day

to Mars

no need to grow
more worthy

burn extra sage

or light one more flame

Her lips descend
when the torrid lust
for future
and past

expires in a fit of
pure exhaustion

and you bless

This Very Moment

As It Is

casting your full-on
gaze to the One

long waiting

and just say

Now

LITTLE BLACK DRESS

Like a little black dress

you can toss
in your suitcase

and wear any place,

good for transits and weather
of every sort

"Please Divine Beloved,

Change me into
One who knows

how the HELL to do this

Let me trust where
You are guiding

and then my Love

Just take me over

ENTIRELY

and lead the way.

Speak for me,
act for me,

I am Yours alone."

(equally fashionable
with a shimmering
necklace
of tears)

UNANSWERED PRAYERS

And the door to my prison dissolved right before me —Ferron

And the time came

finally

when you bowed

with
deep devotion

to every
shuttered

window

and every
sealed gate

blessing

loving

praising
them
for Being

saying

thank you
for stopping me

thank you
for keeping me

from all

I might have

wanted

but do not yet

even

need

ROMANCING THE VOID

when you
stop cramming
your life

with what
matters
little

just to fill
what's empty

you romance
the void

melt to
zero

taste
God's
lips

and draw All
that can make

your heart

take

flight

DIWALI

If you knew
what Love
surrounded you

every moment

Your fears would melt
like icicles

in the
noonday sun

III.

SACRED ASH

SACRED ASH

This offering of
the deepest desires

to the Divine

is the biggest gift

the one that
actually matters

subtle
exquisite

intense beyond
belief

and the hardest
test of all.

But you needn't
deny them
as they arise

They're sacred
after all,

divinely human,

yet you fling them
like dry kindling

into Her fire

so they dance
and crackle
and snap
in Her
flames.

She does
what She will

She knows
every need

And You come
to love that

and to trust

TIGROTTI

One day you will find
that you can go
no further

though you have
come so far

and the trip
is nearly done.

You cannot
go on

you are so tired
your will is gone

so you give up

lay down
in the dirt

on the side of
the mountain

and just pray

Then

the merit of all
past action

bounds
to your side

like a sleek
and rippling

Bengal tiger

to pick you up
lick you clean
and carry you

by the scruff

of your neck

to the

new

time

LOVE POTION #9

This surrender to You
was never
for the timid

Still,
when You said
You wanted

All of me

I swooned
and smiled

like we Bhaktis do

never guessing
what Your

immolation
might actually mean

over and over

You plucked away
each bright bauble

a mad dive-bombing
magpie hell-bent

on but one goal

A trail of your
ink-black feathers
marking

my front door

until my palms
were raw

and cracked

and open

to hold

whatever You

secretly

planned for

all along

SOFT GREEN SHOOTS

No one could
make you

cede the deed
of your Being
to the Goddess Kali

No one

But if you're
on fire to be
Hers

you have
no place to run

Her brick-red ammo
levels you
to rubble

relentless

until

the advent of silence

soft green shoots
blanket the inner
fields

at the end of winter

a thousand
purple crocuses
push through
loamy, sweet soil

each one turning
to the light

of Her sun

INCESSANT PULL

breathe

into the process
however It Is

the incessant
internal pull
like unavoidable
gravity

let the surrender
take you

give yourself over

let it seduce you
into changing
with tongues
of flame

let the melting
into What Is

be an offering

changes are coming
changes are here

yielding
into the vast

desert of

waiting
and
knowing

has already
readied you

for a blessed

birth

IV.

RIPE DARK FRUIT

RIPE DARK FRUIT

Somehow

mysteriously

you wake one day

bowing

goodbye

to all ways

that take everything

and give nothing

your world shifts
on its axis

ripe dark fruit

hangs down from

secret

unseen

trees

AMNESIA

So by now
you know

it's kinda crazy
to keep being told

that Love is
something

to hunt or seek

or win or earn

(or wrap tight
like a python
so you don't
lose)

when in fact
it's busy

streaming through

your own eyes

like high beams

on a dark country road

on those nights
when you

actually

recall

SURFING THE FLOW

Once something is offered

with fullness

to the Divine,

the next actions arise

on their own

The Self takes over

(while the mind watches

 from the shore)

The body makes you wait

or

makes you move

and you simply

KNOW

SILENT SEAT

When you finally take

your calm and silent seat

on the throne

of your own heart

everything begins
to fall into

its proper place

because

You

have

THE STATION OF VENUS

for the next 48 hours
the whole world shudders
to a stop

like a train
shifting direction

the stillness
is deafening

empty horizons
stretch in all
directions

within this void
you could bow to
the lotus feet
of your former self

and kiss
it goodbye

anything that arrives
within this undeterred
landscape
is potent indeed

the wide flat open
prairie

of coming

momentous

change

TABULA RASA

You slipped into my room
each night

to steal my hopes
and dreams
and wishes

and now You scribble
poems

in Your fluid
hand

on the empty white
pages

of my soul.

I'm not complaining.

I never know

what You'll
say

next

V.

UNSHACKLED

ADIEU

suddenly it is easy

to stop banging

on doors that
are bolted

or hearts that
are shut

because
you remember

who You are

And a whole
new world

beckons

alight with ones

to embrace You

and laugh

thank God

You
have
come

UNSHACKLED

Ironically

when you let
the Divine take
the lead

old desires
often
begin to
hatch

and be
fulfilled

anyway

(as a gift
from Love
Herself)
except

now

you're
not

their

slave

HAFIZ THE LOVELORN

So who would
you have been

if that baker's daughter
had not spurned you,

if she had actually

loved you back?

Who would You have been?

You might
have had
no dire need

to plumb
the crags
and rocks

of your own Being

to milk that
gleaming

Love

from your
own bones

no reckless
desperate draw

to mine

the sapphires
gold and
rubies

buried and
abandoned

far

far

inside

What if she had loved
you back?

What if she had loved
you back?

I might not be
adorning

my own body

with Your
bedazzled

gemstones

on this cold
morning

if indeed
she

had

(Dedicated to *Hafez al-Sheraz*, 14th century Persian poet and mystic)

PAST LIVES (ON THE RINGS OF SATURN)

I.

The fact that
some people waltz

straight
into your heart

without any time

in antechambers

or
hallways

is only explainable
by psychosis

or

past

lives

II.

furthermore

the propulsion
away from

or towards

something

or someone

with complete
conviction
probably cannot

be understood

another way

either

III.

you crack the book

back open

right

where you

had stopped,

unable to
recall

exactly

how it all
started

yet hopeless

to forget

or leave

unread

BECKONING THE ECLIPSE

relax

let the early rays of the sun
lick your hands open
to accept and allow

drop your hard

and disappointed shield

invite surprise

besides that, nothing

whatever was planted long ago will
now bloom if it is meant to be

not necessarily tomorrow or today

but in a month or three

let the warmth of the sun
uncoil your tired mind and body
to lure and entice you

open

to receive

TUNING IN

A friend complains
she can't go
find God in India

So I ask,

Why go?

Right now

the breeze runs
Her silky fingers
through your hair

while the sun
kisses and strokes
your arms

your next breath
loves you

and on the radio

the Divine just
crooned,

"Why waste your time?
  You know you're gonna
  be Mine

  You know you're gonna
  be Mine
  You know you're gonna
  be Mine"

  Didn't you notice?

VI.

MORNING BREW

ALLOWING

Sometimes what makes
the ego
suffer

teaches the Soul to fly

like a horse
on the edge
of a rocky, perilous
cliff

with

wings

MORNING BREW

Someone told me she
leads Goddess rituals

saying,

we write our dreams

draw our desires

dance
in a circle

and throw rose petals

everything we
want always

comes true

Ooh, I said

my wish came true
too

MahaKali scared
the living daylights
outta me

She drowned
me in a nearby
river

then chopped me
up and steeped
me

in Her
favorite morning
brew

She said

it tastes

gooood

IDENTITY THEFT

if you think You're a body
then each day brings its share

of indignity
and small disasters

You slide
ever closer
to the Form's

sure departure,

a slowly drooping
flower
a melting icecap.

But if

You are Love

encased for
just a moment

by Matter,

Your Light grows

stronger

evermore free

like an undammed

river

KALI'S MANDALA

When you think life
belongs to you

sand keeps
slipping through your fingers

as you frantically grab
to hold on

no matter what you do
soon enough

all will be gone

but when you give yourself to Love

you become Her wild
art-project mandala

born from shocking, vibrant colors

made to be

birthed and destroyed
birthed and destroyed
birthed and destroyed

Her transient joyous artistry
tossed again
and again

to the rolling

luminous

sea

LIGHTNING

When I finally said

Yes

the sky cracked open

diamonds fell

on treetops

I gave up

no more
bargaining

no more
demands

You clapped

and lightning

pierced the darkness

just Yes

and Yes
and Yes
and Yes

ODE TO THE END OF THE DROUGHT

Bundled up

under gray leaden skies
free from the parched
and brutal sun

the cold rain and sleet
lick my face like a
long lost lover

my body blooms
small pink cactus
flowers

Oh let me walk
in this
forever!

VII.

A JEWEL IN YOUR MOUTH

EVENING MEDITATION

At the far side
of these desires

is a freefall

into

Love

when you release
the handful of dust

you clutch so tightly

you melt into the
starless void

which absorbs
all It touches

and dissolve into

the dark crystalline
decanter

of God's
own mind

OAKLAND CHAPEL

I sit attended by
fern and bougainvillea

the canvas on the ceiling
snaps and rustles

in the breeze
from the bay

sparrows chirp loudly

while jasmine and gardenia
hang heavy in the air

the room glows
phosphorous gold
as the afternoon sun
paints a window

and the mind
cannot
help

but
surrender.

From deep within
my silence

a radio on the street
blasts Steve Winwood

Higher Love

LAST DANCE

In Memory of my Mom, Debby Barkan Silver

I came to see you

hanging in
the balance

and began to rub
those tender feet

that once adored
to dance

searing
a final image
into my Being

your fine hair
blonde and wild
as a daikini

your body almost
weightless

almost done

then suddenly
I was on the floor

before You

my cheek pressed
into those arches
narrow and
small

my tears wetting
your broken tiny body

praying
for a better way

to thank you

for all
You had

given

and all
You had

done

TAKE-OFF

The other day I watched
a snowy egret
perched on a ragged
wooden fence

along a nearby marsh

She stood
a long, long time

calm and impassive

her wings half-open
like a silken fringed white tallis

for prayer

And then at the decided moment

she raised them higher

and was gone

ENDGAME

And in the end,

but one finish line
one goal

no matter what
was fervently

awaited
or sought

You were
the radiant God
and Goddess

all along

poised in the heart
of Your own
galaxy

pretending

to be a
struggling

human form

LONG BEACH LUNATION

A stroll in pale windy
moonlight

your newborn mind
hugged to you

like a swaddled infant

or a sapling
with the barest roots
that the next gust

might take down

The Divine is All
so obvious now

So you walk

braced against the wind

washed by the moon

checking yourself
often

like a jewel you hide
in your mouth

to smuggle
across the border

between worlds

Other Books by Tosha Silver

Outrageous Openness: Letting the Divine Take the Lead

Outrageous Openness opens the door to a profound truth: By allowing the Divine to lead the way, we can finally put down the heavy load of hopes, fears, and opinions about how things should be. We learn how to be guided to take the right actions at the right time, and to enjoy the spectacular show that is our life.

"Tosha Silver is an empathetic guide along the ever-present seam between the everyday and the sacred, letting us know that we can pull a thread of aliveness for ourselves at any time."

— Mark Nepo, author of *The Endless Practice* and *Seven Thousand Ways to Listen*

"In a marketplace filled with lackluster spirituality books, this book sparkles with truth. Through touching personal stories, potent insights and holy humor, Tosha Silver reminds us that the only way to truly live is hand in hand, heart to heart, and hip bump to hip bump with the Divine."

— Sera Beak author of *Red Hot and Holy: A Heretic's Love Story*

Change Me Prayers: The Hidden Power of Spiritual Surrender

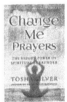

In this sequel to *Outrageous Openness*, Tosha Silver, with her characteristic mix of passion and humor, shows how to embrace transformation from the inside out. Covering a variety of topics — from work and finances to love and self-worth — *Change Me Prayers* shows how to truly surrender to a Divine plan in the most joyous and uplifting way.

"*Change Me Prayers* has, quite frankly, changed my life. I have learned what spiritual surrender really is. This potent path of love and guidance has helped me recover from grief, pain, and loss while opening me more fully to the joy and delight of life."

— Christiane Northrup, M.D., New York Times bestselling author of *Goddesses Never Age: The Secret Prescription for Radiance, Joy, and Wellbeing*

"Her prayers let our connection to the divine be intimate & immediate, so we can experience divine love when we need to most- right in the midst of our everyday panic & dread, right when we might shut down, love reaches farther instead."

— Meggan Watterson, *REVEAL: A Sacred Manual For Getting Spiritually Naked*

Join the "Living Outrageous Openness" Forum

The *Living Outrageous Openness* forum is an ongoing program designed to help you ACTIVELY live the ideas in OO so inspired actions and solutions arise on their own at the right time.

⤳ You learn how to truly let the Inner Divine lead in even the most challenging situations.

⤳ Miracles arrive that you never could have imagined.

⤳ And most importantly, you start to remember who You actually are.

Our culture is so often about efforting, chasing and grasping, this is for people ready to let Love lead.

People ask HOW to apply the ideas in these books to daily life: in relationships, work, health business, loss, and everything else. Luckily, learning to invite the Divine into one's everyday life is a muscle that grows stronger with time.

It just takes practice.

Visit www.toshasilver.com to learn more.

About the Cover

If you've read *Outrageous Openness* or *Change Me Prayers* you know I love the many forms of the Divine, from Jesus to Guadalupe to Quan Yin to Lord Ganesh. But MahaKali, the transcendent Hindu Goddess who rules death, rebirth, and time itself, captures my heart every single day. Yet She especially is often feared, misunderstood and maligned in our culture!

In fact, She is a protective, compassionate Mother to those who long to know Her, and who offer Her their hearts with full devotion. As the slayer of demons, both physical and spiritual, She awakens us from the sleepwalk of delusions, delivering us to our true authentic Selves. According to the Hindu cosmology, we live in Her era, the Kali Yuga.

Plus, being connected to the sign Scorpio, She is often a favorite of Plutonic sorts like myself. With twelve points in my own chart all touching Pluto, I cannot help but adore Her. Perhaps you were drawn for a similar reason?

Jai Kali Ma!